MONS[...]

Lady Monster and the garden

27

Monster and Lady Monster are out walking in the city streets.
You can tell it's a big city because there are tall buildings and hardly any trees at all.
It's very busy.
The people are hurrying from place to place.
Monster and Lady Monster look at all the sights. They talk about different things.

"What's this?" says Monster.
"What's this garden doing right in the middle of the city? It looks like a farm."
"It *is* a farm!" says Lady Monster.
"Look at the lettuce and those tomatoes. What beauties!"

Monster and Lady Monster talk to
the city farmers.
"You can have a garden, too, if you work
hard," says the man.
"You need energy and a lot of time.
First, you have to buy some seeds.
Then, you have to plant them.
You have to use plenty of water and let the sun
shine on them."

“This watermelon was once a very tiny seed,” says the farmer. “Now look at it. And I bet it will be delicious.”

Monster and Lady Monster are amazed. Maybe they could grow watermelon that big. Then they could eat it—their very own watermelon.

"Let's go home," says Lady Monster.
"Let's look at your back garden."
Monster and Lady Monster rush home so fast.
They are in such a hurry to start their own garden.

Monster's back garden is a mess!
There are old tyres everywhere.
It looks like a rubbish dump.
Nothing has ever been planted there, so nothing grows.

"Oh boy, this is an awful mess," says Lady Monster.
"How are we ever going to get this clean?"
Monster and Lady Monster wonder if they will ever be able to make the place look beautiful.

They decide to try.

Monster and Lady Monster and the little boy and the little girl start digging up the back garden.
Monster has a spade and Lady Monster is using a hoe. The hoe helps turn over the soil so it won't be all lumpy.
Then you can plant the seeds.

They will have to decide what to plant.

Monster and Lady Monster visit a garden shop to buy seeds.
They look at all the packets of seeds.

Monster and Lady Monster can't decide what to plant.
It takes a very long time at the shop.
They talk about each seed.
Finally, they choose.

Monster and Lady Monster start planting
the seeds.
They push the seeds into the ground
and cover them over with soil.

Every day, Monster and Lady Monster look out of the window.
They look at each marker.
They wonder when all the plants will start to grow.

But nothing is happening. It takes a lot of sun and water and time for the seeds to push above the soil.

One day, the little boy and the little girl come running.
"Come on, Monster," they shout.
"Something is growing in our garden."
Monster and Lady Monster go to have a look.

It's a sad sight.
The seeds have started to grow,
but something has happened.
The leaves have been nibbled.
The stems have been chewed.
It is very sad.

Monster can hardly believe his eyes.
He is very upset.
He wonders what is going on.

Monster and Lady Monster realise
there are animals all around
who are eating their plants.

"We need a way to scare them off,"
says Monster.
"Try banners," says Lady Monster.
"How about a radio?" says the little boy.
"Maybe we can frighten the animals away."

They don't.
The next day, more plants have been eaten.
It looks as if the plants are shrinking.
This is serious.

Monster and Lady Monster decide to build a fence. It is made of wire.
"Maybe this fence will keep the animals out of the garden," says Monster.
Lady Monster thinks it's worth trying.

But it doesn't help.
The animals are eating up all the things in the garden.
This is very discouraging.
Monster had thought the plants would be really big by now.
"This is getting us nowhere," he says.

Then, Lady Monster has an idea.
She knows they have to do something.
Lady Monster tells Monster her plan.
Her idea sounds very good.

Monster and Lady Monster and the little boy
and the little girl start making
big statues of themselves.
They use wire, paper and glue.
They make papier mâché.

The figures look just like Monster
and Lady Monster.
They're big and scary looking.

The little boy and the little girl
look real, too.
This might be a really good trick.
These statues might scare away
the animals.
"I wonder if this
is going to work,"
says Monster.

The figures are just like scarecrows.
They can stay outside all night.
They sit at a table right next to the garden.
There is a light over the table where
the statues are sitting.
If the animals think the people are
real, maybe they won't come into the garden.
Maybe the statues will frighten them away.

The idea works!
When the animals see the statues,
they run away.
No animals eat any of the plants!
All the food in the garden is saved.
Nothing has been nibbled.
Everything will be able to grow just right.

When the plants are ready, Monster and Lady Monster and the little boy and the little girl taste them.
They have a feast.
The vegetables taste delicious.

All the hard work has paid off.
Everyone is very pleased.